THE NEW NATURAL

A SURVEY OF BRITISH N

F U N L

The aim of this series is to interest the general reader in the wildlife
of Britain by recapturing the enquiring spirit of the old naturalists.
The editors believe that the natural pride of the British public
in the native flora, fauna and fungi, to which must be added
concern for their conservation, is best fostered
by maintaining a high standard of accuracy
combined with clarity of exposition
in presenting the results
of modern scientific
research.

First Period wares (1926 to c1932/33). The souvenir ashtray has the town name of 'Southsea' painted on the side, and was probably decorated by Reginald Davies, (see page 3 for detail of image).

Vases, H.14.5 cm

The two jugs are Second Period wares (c1932/33 to1938). Tallest, H.19.5 cm

The Totland Pottery

— Kenneth A Scotcher
The Broadway, Totland Bay
1957 to c1987

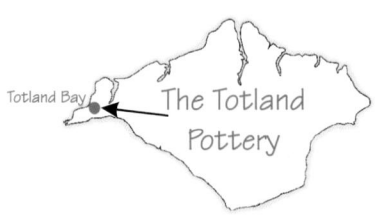

pottery mark — variations occur

KEN SCOTCHER ran THE TOTLAND POTTERY for Joe Lester for a year before taking over the business himself in 1958, from which date he used his own back stamp.

Producing ware similar to Joe, Ken continued to use white earthenware clay and bright colours under a clear gloss glaze, making mainly wheel-thrown, easily portable items for holiday-makers.

In the early 1960s, Ken's sister Barbara started work at the pottery. Ken taught her various decorating techniques and she remained as decorator for 25 years, using the popular methods of banding and sgraffito.

Admirers and collectors of ceramics alike will easily recognise The Totland Pottery wares without even having to check the back stamp on much of the finely thrown, precisely decorated ware.

Unusual pieces include decoration with quirky animal subjects (see pages 36 and 37), and historical figures; large thrown pots; and non-standard colourway items.

The Totland Pottery's wares are easily identifiable by the distinctive colours and decoration used by Ken Scotcher and his sister, Barbara Joan Stokes.

Collection of the authors

Wheel-thrown pin dish with a sgraffito-decorated bird in the style of a 'Barnett Bird'. The original Barnett Bird design was created by Joe Lester's principal decorator/designer Miss Ruby McNeill Slade, and many variations have subsequently evolved. The bird was named after Lady Isobel Barnett, a popular panellist on the BBC TV show *'What's My Line?'* during the 1950s, and well-known for her extravagant style of hats. She was a visitor at 'ideal home style' exhibitions in Britain where Joe Lester had a stand entitled *'The Potter and his Wheel'*. *Historical note: Interestingly, 'Barnet Fair' is the British slang for 'hair'.*

This particular piece was made by Ken Scotcher during the first year of potting in his own studio whilst still working for Joe Lester. It has the standard Joe Lester mark (see page 28) with 'Hand Made' above, and 'in Totland' below an outline of the Isle of Wight. Used from 1957 to 1958.

D.12 cm

Above Wheel-thrown pin dish with sgraffito decoration. Like the Barnett Bird opposite, it is more unusual to see an example decorated with an animal subject. Ken Scotcher's wares were invariably decorated with coloured banding and a single band of sgraffito motifs or patterns, as seen right and on page 35. Again, the dish above was made during Ken's first year on The Broadway.

D.12 cm

Right
Drainer and bowl.
Largest, D.20 cm

The Ventnor
Pottery Studio – John Reilly

pottery mark – variations occur

JOHN REILLY is an artist. He worked for Joe Lester at Freshwater, mainly as a decorator, before they set up a pottery together in the village of Niton in 1955.

In 1960 the partnership amicably dissolved and John opened his own ceramic studio in Ventnor, with a view to producing primarily paintings, and decorative ceramic wall plaques and tiles. Painting on canvas was John's first love, and eventually he set up a home studio. His daughter Kim, with whom he worked for a while, took over the pottery until 1985. (Kim works today under the name of 'Metamorphics'.)

John's early thrown white earthenware pieces were mainly decorated in Joe Lester's style. Later shapes were cast, often adorned with colourful characters such as exotic birds, lions, and sea horses. The sun-kissed palette of his ceramic panels, wall plaques, and dishes, were a prelude to his now ineffable style of oil painting.

 Unusual pieces include large all-over decorated wheel-thrown pots; vibrant tiled panels and plaques of animal studies, nature and landscapes, in a riot of dazzling colours.

One of the unique tiled wall panels by John Reilly.
The tile width measures approximately 15 cm.
Sea horses feature strongly with the Island, but a common theme
seen through John's work at Ventnor is parables from the Bible.

Photo courtesy Steve Wake LRPS

Slip-cast wall plaque with decorative quirky owl.
John Reilly's characters are always colourful
and often humorous.

H.26.5 cm

Collection of Mr D Morey
Photo courtesy Steve Wake LRPS

Individually decorated tiles were also very popular.
When strolling along Island streets, the observant person
may spot house names or numbers in the form
of tiles decorated by John Reilly.

W.15 cm

Collection of the authors

Some pottery jargon

YOU MAY OR MAY NOT have come across a few pottery terms used in this book that are unfamiliar. If you have, then for your reference a list of some pottery words used, together with a brief explanation of what they mean, is detailed below.

Banding – decorating a pot by applying different glaze colours or slips while the pot is revolving on the wheel.

Cast – pottery wares that have been made by pouring liquid clay (known as 'slip') into a prepared mould, and left to dry before releasing from the mould.

Chattering – either 1. A form of decoration using a hand tool to mark the clay as the pot revolves on the wheel; or 2. A surface irregularity fault.

Earthenware – low-fired pottery made from a clay which, when fired once, is still porous and needs to be glaze fired before it can hold water. Usually fired to temperatures between 1000°C and 1150°C.

Maiolica – a form of decoration on tin-glazed earthenware where oxides and stains are applied, usually with a brush, to an unfired glazed surface.

Paperclay – clay slip mixed with paper pulp, and sometimes other additives. Wet pieces of paperclay can be added to dry pieces and vice versa before firing, when the paper burns away.

Porcelain – is usually white in colour when fired, often translucent, vitreous and non-porous. Usually glaze fired to a temperature between 1220°C and 1450°C.

Sgraffito – a method of decorating which involves scratching a design with a sharp tool through slip or glaze, to reveal the clay or colour beneath.

Stoneware – pottery made with clay which, when glaze fired, is non-porous and vitreous. Usually fired to temperatures between 1200°C and 1300°C.

Throwing – a method of making where a pot is pulled up from a lump of plastic clay, and shaped by hand and fingers on a revolving potter's wheel. The wheel can be driven either by electricity, foot (ie a kick wheel), by hand, or with a stick.

Vectis Ware – pottery made on the Island in Roman times termed as 'Vectis ware' as the Romans referred to the Isle of Wight as the Island of 'Vectis'.

Wax-resist – liquid wax is brushed onto a pattern marked on a biscuit-fired pot. The pot is then dipped or sprayed with glaze which is resisted by the wax, and when fired the wax burns away leaving the design.

Things you might like to know about

NOW YOU'VE HAD A TASTE of Isle of Wight pottery, you may like to visit places to either view old or new pots, or to perhaps purchase work being made today. With this in mind, we thought a list of some Island galleries and museums might be useful, not forgetting of course a few potters to visit.

It's always a good idea to phone before making a journey to visit any of those listed below. You may need to check opening times and/or to see if an entry fee applies. Also, depending on your interest, you may need to find out the type of pottery being exhibited or available to purchase. The Island telephone code for all numbers detailed is 01983 (except mobiles).

GALLERIES
usually stocking contemporary Isle of Wight pottery

Flip Flop
9 St Thomas' Square, Newport
T • 537437
W • www.flipflopshop.co.uk

Quay Arts
Sea Street, Newport
T • 822490
W • www.quayarts.org

Unique Crafts Gallery
5 Foreland Road, Bembridge
T • 874173

Wight Light Gallery
1A High Street, Ventnor
T • 857097
W • www.wightlightgallery.co.uk

Yarmouth Gallery
High Street, Yarmouth
T • 760226
W • www.yarmouthgalleryiw.com

A FEW POTTERIES TO VISIT

Remember! – 1. Opening times may vary throughout the
year, so it's a good idea to phone first, and;
2. Some potters receive visitors 'by appointment only' ('b.a.o'.)
– a telephone call is therefore essential.

Molly Attrill
Mersley Farm, Newchurch

T • 862028/731116
E • mollyattrill@mersley.fsnet.co.uk

Andrew Bristow
Bonchurch Pottery
Shore Road, Bonchurch

T • 854445
W • www.bonchurchpottery.co.uk

Ceramic Crafts
Arreton Barns Craft Village, Arreton

T • 530344
W • www.ceramiccrafts.com

Chessell Pottery Barns
Brook Road, Chessell, Nr Calbourne

T • 531248
W • www.chessellpotterybarns.co.uk

Andrew Dowden – 'b.a.o.'

T • 867505
E • ilonatracey@hotmail.com

Margaret Hodge – 'b.a.o.'
Norton, Nr Yarmouth

T • 761121

Lodestone Pottery – 'b.a.o.'

T • 760235
E • lodestone.pot@virgin.net

Sue Paraskeva – 'b.a.o.'
Jubilee Stores, The Quay, Newport

M • 07968 336485
W • www.sueparaskeva.co.uk

Kim Reilly – 'b.a.o.'
'Metamorphics Pottery'

T • 853612

Remember! Some potters receive visitors
'by appointment only' ('b.a.o'.)
— a telephone call is therefore essential.

Brother Alexander Tingay
Quarr Abbey Pottery, (Shop Only)
Quarr Abbey, Binstead

T • 882420 Ext 5258
E • pottery@quarrabbey.co.uk

Lis Toft 'Hotpots' — 'b.a.o.'
Jubilee Stores, The Quay, Newport

T • 756382
E • listoft@btopenworld.com

Sally Woodford — 'b.a.o.'
Bembridge

T • 873339

PLACES TO SEE
ancient and/or historical pots
Please Note — Entry fees apply!

Brading Roman Villa
Morton Old Road, Brading

T • 406223
W • www.bradingromanvilla.org.uk

Carisbrooke Castle Museum
Carisbrooke Castle, Nr Newport

T • 523112
W • www.carisbrookecastlemuseum.org.uk

Museum of Island History
The Guildhall, High Street, Newport

T • 823366
W • www.iwight.com

Newport Roman Villa
Cypress Road, Newport

T • 529720
W • www.iwight.com

Further reading

WE HOPE YOU'VE ENJOYED this very brief look at the ceramic treasures on our beautiful sunshine Isle. You might even have found an item of pottery to keep as a souvenir. If your appetite has been whet and you'd like to learn more about Isle of Wight potters and potteries, past and present, then you may be interested in reading the first I.O.W. pottery book 'A Century of Ceramics' – A Selection of 20th Century Potters and Potteries in the Isle of Wight.

Published in 2005 (text copyright Lisa Dowden), the book looks at 27 Island ceramic makers in more depth, including the eight potters featured in this book. With 256 glossy pages in full colour throughout, it also includes an overview of ancient Island pottery, location maps, and a comprehensive list of pottery terms used in the book. There are over 350 col/b&w images, including potters' marks, and a directory of some contemporary Island makers, with details of their work and how to contact them.

The book size is 21.5 cm wide (8½ inches), by 28 cm high (11 inches), and is available direct from us, and selected outlets, in paperback (isbn 0-9548745-1-X) priced at £28. Hardback limited edition copies (from a print-run of 500, with signed and numbered bookplate), are still available direct from us priced at £35 (isbn 0-9548745-0-1). Postage and packing applies to both paperback and hardback copies. ('A Century of Ceramics' is UK distribution only.)

If you'd like further details, you can phone us on: 01983 867505, email: ilonatracey@hotmail.com, or write to us at: Buttercup Cottage Books, PO Box 90, Sandown, PO36 6AP.

an Isle of Wight souvenir book

At the end of a rainbow . . .
HISTORICAL
Isle of Wight Pottery

. . . even further reading,
Articles & Chapters . . .

'Isle of Wight Handcraft Pottery'
Article: Journal of the
Northern Ceramic Society, Volume 11
by Dr N T Cooke

'Roman Wight – A Guide Catalogue'
by David Tomalin (I.W.C.)

'Excavations at Carisbrooke Castle
Isle of Wight 1921–1996'
by C J Young
(Wessex Archaeology in conjunction with English Heritage)

Thanks for reading!